OUR BUCKET LIST

Allison: Thank

May you always

seek new adventures

together!

Merry Christmas
2018

Lisa

Activity

Page

Done!

Activity	Page	Done!

Activity   Page   Done!

Activity	Page	Done!

Activity   Page   Done!

Date Completed:_____

Overall Rating: ☆ ☆ ☆ ☆ ☆

Description:

_____
_____
_____
_____
_____

Why we wanted to do this:

_____
_____
_____

Thoughts/Memories:

_____
_____
_____
_____
_____
_____
_____
_____
_____
_____

_____

Date Completed:_____

Overall Rating: ☆ ☆ ☆ ☆ ☆

Description:

_____

_____

_____

_____

_____

Why we wanted to do this:

_____

_____

_____

Thoughts/Memories:

_____

_____

_____

_____

_____

_____

_____

_____

_____

_____

⟫⟫⟫———➤ ⟫⟫⟫———➤ ⟫⟫⟫———➤ ⟫⟫⟫———➤

Date Completed:_____

Overall Rating: ☆ ☆ ☆ ☆ ☆

Description:

_____
_____
_____
_____
_____

Why we wanted to do this:

_____
_____
_____

Thoughts/Memories:

_____
_____
_____
_____
_____
_____
_____
_____
_____
_____

≫≫≫———➤ ≫≫≫———➤ ≫≫≫———➤ ≫≫≫———➤

Date Completed:_____

Overall Rating: ☆ ☆ ☆ ☆ ☆

Description:

_____
_____
_____
_____
_____

Why we wanted to do this:

_____
_____
_____

Thoughts/Memories:

_____
_____
_____
_____
_____
_____
_____
_____
_____
_____
_____

》》》——➤ 》》》——➤ 》》》——➤ 》》》——➤

Date Completed: _____

Overall Rating: ☆ ☆ ☆ ☆ ☆

Description:
_____
_____
_____
_____
_____

Why we wanted to do this:
_____
_____
_____

Thoughts/Memories:
_____
_____
_____
_____
_____
_____
_____
_____
_____
_____

>>>———➤ >>>———➤ >>>———➤ >>>———➤

Date Completed: _____

Overall Rating: ☆ ☆ ☆ ☆ ☆

Description:

_____

_____

_____

_____

_____

Why we wanted to do this:

_____

_____

_____

Thoughts/Memories:

_____

_____

_____

_____

_____

_____

_____

_____

_____

_____

》》》————→ 》》》————→ 》》》————→ 》》》————→

Date Completed:_____

Overall Rating: ☆ ☆ ☆ ☆ ☆

Description:

_____
_____
_____
_____
_____

Why we wanted to do this:

_____
_____
_____

Thoughts/Memories:

_____
_____
_____
_____
_____
_____
_____
_____
_____
_____
_____

Date Completed:_____

Overall Rating: ☆ ☆ ☆ ☆ ☆

Description:

_____

_____

_____

_____

_____

Why we wanted to do this:

_____

_____

_____

Thoughts/Memories:

_____

_____

_____

_____

_____

_____

_____

_____

_____

_____

》》》———➤ 》》》———➤ 》》》———➤ 》》》———➤

Date Completed:_____

Overall Rating: ☆ ☆ ☆ ☆ ☆

Description:

_____

_____

_____

_____

_____

Why we wanted to do this:

_____

_____

_____

Thoughts/Memories:

_____

_____

_____

_____

_____

_____

_____

_____

_____

_____

》》》———➤ 》》》———➤ 》》》———➤ 》》》———➤

Date Completed: _____

Overall Rating: ☆ ☆ ☆ ☆ ☆

Description:

_____
_____
_____
_____
_____

Why we wanted to do this:

_____
_____
_____

Thoughts/Memories:

_____
_____
_____
_____
_____
_____
_____
_____
_____
_____
_____

≫≫—➤ ≫≫—➤ ≫≫—➤ ≫≫—➤

Date Completed:_____

Overall Rating: ☆ ☆ ☆ ☆ ☆

Description:

_____
_____
_____
_____
_____

Why we wanted to do this:

_____
_____
_____

Thoughts/Memories:

_____
_____
_____
_____
_____
_____
_____
_____
_____
_____

≫≫➤   ≫≫➤   ≫≫➤   ≫≫➤

Date Completed: _____

Overall Rating: ☆ ☆ ☆ ☆ ☆

Description:

_____
_____
_____
_____
_____

Why we wanted to do this:

_____
_____
_____

Thoughts/Memories:

_____
_____
_____
_____
_____
_____
_____
_____
_____
_____
_____

Date Completed: _____

Overall Rating: ☆ ☆ ☆ ☆ ☆

Description:

_____
_____
_____
_____
_____

Why we wanted to do this:

_____
_____
_____

Thoughts/Memories:

_____
_____
_____
_____
_____
_____
_____
_____
_____
_____

>>>———➤ >>>———➤ >>>———➤ >>>———➤

Date Completed:_____

Overall Rating: ☆ ☆ ☆ ☆ ☆

Description:

_____
_____
_____
_____
_____

Why we wanted to do this:

_____
_____
_____

Thoughts/Memories:

_____
_____
_____
_____
_____
_____
_____
_____
_____
_____
_____

⟫⟩→ ⟫⟩→ ⟫⟩→ ⟫⟩→

Date Completed:_____

Overall Rating: ☆ ☆ ☆ ☆ ☆

Description:

_____
_____
_____
_____
_____

Why we wanted to do this:

_____
_____
_____

Thoughts/Memories:

_____
_____
_____
_____
_____
_____
_____
_____
_____
_____
_____

>>>———➤ >>>———➤ >>>———➤ >>>———➤

Date Completed: _____

Overall Rating: ☆ ☆ ☆ ☆ ☆

Description:

_____
_____
_____
_____
_____

Why we wanted to do this:

_____
_____
_____

Thoughts/Memories:

_____
_____
_____
_____
_____
_____
_____
_____
_____
_____

»»—➤ »»—➤ »»—➤ »»—➤

Date Completed:_____

Overall Rating: ☆ ☆ ☆ ☆ ☆

Description:

_____

_____

_____

_____

_____

Why we wanted to do this:

_____

_____

_____

Thoughts/Memories:

_____

_____

_____

_____

_____

_____

_____

_____

_____

_____

>>>——➤ >>>——➤ >>>——➤ >>>——➤

Date Completed:_____

Overall Rating: ☆ ☆ ☆ ☆ ☆

Description:

_____

_____

_____

_____

_____

Why we wanted to do this:

_____

_____

_____

Thoughts/Memories:

_____

_____

_____

_____

_____

_____

_____

_____

_____

_____

>>>———➤ >>>———➤ >>>———➤ >>>———➤

Date Completed:_____

Overall Rating: ☆ ☆ ☆ ☆ ☆

Description:

_____
_____
_____
_____
_____

Why we wanted to do this:

_____
_____
_____

Thoughts/Memories:

_____
_____
_____
_____
_____
_____
_____
_____
_____
_____

»»———➤ »»———➤ »»———➤ »»———➤

Date Completed:_____

Overall Rating: ☆ ☆ ☆ ☆ ☆

Description:

_____
_____
_____
_____
_____

Why we wanted to do this:

_____
_____
_____

Thoughts/Memories:

_____
_____
_____
_____
_____
_____
_____
_____
_____
_____

》》》———➤ 》》》———➤ 》》》———➤ 》》》———➤

Date Completed:_____

Overall Rating: ☆ ☆ ☆ ☆ ☆

Description:

_____
_____
_____
_____
_____

Why we wanted to do this:

_____
_____
_____

Thoughts/Memories:

_____
_____
_____
_____
_____
_____
_____
_____
_____
_____

Date Completed:_____

Overall Rating: ☆ ☆ ☆ ☆ ☆

Description:

_____
_____
_____
_____
_____

Why we wanted to do this:

_____
_____
_____

Thoughts/Memories:

_____
_____
_____
_____
_____
_____
_____
_____
_____
_____
_____

>>>————➤ >>>————➤ >>>————➤ >>>————➤

Date Completed:_____

Overall Rating: ☆ ☆ ☆ ☆ ☆

Description:

_____

_____

_____

_____

_____

Why we wanted to do this:

_____

_____

_____

Thoughts/Memories:

_____

_____

_____

_____

_____

_____

_____

_____

_____

_____

≫≫⟶ ≫≫⟶ ≫≫⟶ ≫≫⟶

Date Completed:_____

Overall Rating: ☆ ☆ ☆ ☆ ☆

Description:

_____
_____
_____
_____
_____

Why we wanted to do this:

_____
_____
_____

Thoughts/Memories:

_____
_____
_____
_____
_____
_____
_____
_____
_____
_____

»»» ——➤ »»» ——➤ »»» ——➤ »»» ——➤

Date Completed:_____

Overall Rating: ☆ ☆ ☆ ☆ ☆

Description:

_____

_____

_____

_____

_____

Why we wanted to do this:

_____

_____

_____

Thoughts/Memories:

_____

_____

_____

_____

_____

_____

_____

_____

_____

_____

Date Completed:_____

Overall Rating: ☆ ☆ ☆ ☆ ☆

Description:

_____
_____
_____
_____
_____

Why we wanted to do this:

_____
_____
_____

Thoughts/Memories:

_____
_____
_____
_____
_____
_____
_____
_____
_____
_____
_____

⇛⟶ ⇛⟶ ⇛⟶ ⇛⟶

Date Completed:_____

Overall Rating: ☆ ☆ ☆ ☆ ☆

Description:

_____

_____

_____

_____

_____

Why we wanted to do this:

_____

_____

_____

Thoughts/Memories:

_____

_____

_____

_____

_____

_____

_____

_____

_____

_____

≫≫→ ≫≫→ ≫≫→ ≫≫→

Date Completed:_____

Overall Rating: ☆ ☆ ☆ ☆ ☆

Description:

_____
_____
_____
_____
_____

Why we wanted to do this:

_____
_____
_____

Thoughts/Memories:

_____
_____
_____
_____
_____
_____
_____
_____
_____
_____
_____

》》》———➤ 》》》———➤ 》》》———➤ 》》》———➤

Date Completed:_____

Overall Rating: ☆ ☆ ☆ ☆ ☆

Description:

_____
_____
_____
_____
_____

Why we wanted to do this:

_____
_____
_____

Thoughts/Memories:

_____
_____
_____
_____
_____
_____
_____
_____
_____
_____

⟫⟫⟫——➤ ⟫⟫⟫——➤ ⟫⟫⟫——➤ ⟫⟫⟫——➤

_____

Date Completed:_____

Overall Rating: ☆ ☆ ☆ ☆ ☆

Description:

_____
_____
_____
_____
_____

Why we wanted to do this:

_____
_____
_____

Thoughts/Memories:

_____
_____
_____
_____
_____
_____
_____
_____
_____
_____

»»»———➤ »»»———➤ »»»———➤ »»»———➤

Date Completed:_____

Overall Rating: ☆ ☆ ☆ ☆ ☆

Description:

_____
_____
_____
_____
_____

Why we wanted to do this:

_____
_____
_____

Thoughts/Memories:

_____
_____
_____
_____
_____
_____
_____
_____
_____
_____

»»——➤ »»——➤ »»——➤ »»——➤

Date Completed: _____

Overall Rating: ☆ ☆ ☆ ☆ ☆

Description:

_____

_____

_____

_____

_____

Why we wanted to do this:

_____

_____

_____

Thoughts/Memories:

_____

_____

_____

_____

_____

_____

_____

_____

_____

_____

≫≫⟶ ≫≫⟶ ≫≫⟶ ≫≫⟶

Date Completed:_____

Overall Rating: ☆ ☆ ☆ ☆ ☆

Description:

_____
_____
_____
_____
_____

Why we wanted to do this:

_____
_____
_____

Thoughts/Memories:

_____
_____
_____
_____
_____
_____
_____
_____
_____
_____
_____

»»»————➤ »»»————➤ »»»————➤ »»»————➤

Date Completed:_____

Overall Rating: ☆ ☆ ☆ ☆ ☆

Description:

_____

_____

_____

_____

_____

Why we wanted to do this:

_____

_____

_____

Thoughts/Memories:

_____

_____

_____

_____

_____

_____

_____

_____

_____

_____

>>>——→ >>>——→ >>>——→ >>>——→

Date Completed: _____

Overall Rating: ☆ ☆ ☆ ☆ ☆

Description:

_____
_____
_____
_____
_____

Why we wanted to do this:

_____
_____
_____

Thoughts/Memories:

_____
_____
_____
_____
_____
_____
_____
_____
_____
_____

≫≫→ ≫≫→ ≫≫→ ≫≫→

Date Completed:_____

Overall Rating: ☆ ☆ ☆ ☆ ☆

Description:

_____
_____
_____
_____
_____

Why we wanted to do this:

_____
_____
_____

Thoughts/Memories:

_____
_____
_____
_____
_____
_____
_____
_____
_____
_____

➤➤➤———➤ ➤➤➤———➤ ➤➤➤———➤ ➤➤➤———➤

Date Completed:_____

Overall Rating: ☆ ☆ ☆ ☆ ☆

Description:

_____
_____
_____
_____
_____

Why we wanted to do this:

_____
_____
_____

Thoughts/Memories:

_____
_____
_____
_____
_____
_____
_____
_____
_____
_____
_____

≫≫—→ ≫≫—→ ≫≫—→ ≫≫—→

Date Completed:_____

Overall Rating: ☆ ☆ ☆ ☆ ☆

Description:

_____

_____

_____

_____

_____

Why we wanted to do this:

_____

_____

_____

Thoughts/Memories:

_____

_____

_____

_____

_____

_____

_____

_____

_____

_____

»»———➤ »»———➤ »»———➤ »»———➤

Date Completed: _____

Overall Rating: ☆ ☆ ☆ ☆ ☆

Description:

_____
_____
_____
_____
_____

Why we wanted to do this:

_____
_____
_____

Thoughts/Memories:

_____
_____
_____
_____
_____
_____
_____
_____
_____
_____

>>>⟶ >>>⟶ >>>⟶ >>>⟶

Date Completed:_____

Overall Rating: ☆ ☆ ☆ ☆ ☆

Description:

_____

_____

_____

_____

_____

Why we wanted to do this:

_____

_____

_____

Thoughts/Memories:

_____

_____

_____

_____

_____

_____

_____

_____

_____

_____

》》》———➤ 》》》———➤ 》》》———➤ 》》》———➤

Date Completed: _____

Overall Rating: ☆ ☆ ☆ ☆ ☆

Description:

_____
_____
_____
_____
_____

Why we wanted to do this:

_____
_____
_____

Thoughts/Memories:

_____
_____
_____
_____
_____
_____
_____
_____
_____
_____

Date Completed:_____

Overall Rating: ☆ ☆ ☆ ☆ ☆

Description:

_____
_____
_____
_____
_____

Why we wanted to do this:

_____
_____
_____

Thoughts/Memories:

_____
_____
_____
_____
_____
_____
_____
_____
_____
_____

⇉⟶ ⇉⟶ ⇉⟶ ⇉⟶

Date Completed:_____

Overall Rating: ☆ ☆ ☆ ☆ ☆

Description:

_____
_____
_____
_____
_____

Why we wanted to do this:

_____
_____
_____

Thoughts/Memories:

_____
_____
_____
_____
_____
_____
_____
_____
_____
_____

Date Completed: _____

Overall Rating: ☆ ☆ ☆ ☆ ☆

Description:

_____

_____

_____

_____

_____

Why we wanted to do this:

_____

_____

_____

Thoughts/Memories:

_____

_____

_____

_____

_____

_____

_____

_____

_____

_____

_____

»»———➤ »»———➤ »»———➤ »»———➤

Date Completed:_____

Overall Rating: ☆ ☆ ☆ ☆ ☆

Description:

_____
_____
_____
_____
_____

Why we wanted to do this:

_____
_____
_____

Thoughts/Memories:

_____
_____
_____
_____
_____
_____
_____
_____
_____
_____

➤➤➤ ➤ ➤➤➤ ➤ ➤➤➤ ➤ ➤➤➤ ➤

Date Completed:_____

Overall Rating: ☆ ☆ ☆ ☆ ☆

Description:

_____

_____

_____

_____

_____

Why we wanted to do this:

_____

_____

_____

Thoughts/Memories:

_____

_____

_____

_____

_____

_____

_____

_____

_____

_____

_____

»»»————➤   »»»————➤   »»»————➤   »»»————➤

Date Completed:_____

Overall Rating: ☆ ☆ ☆ ☆ ☆

Description:

_____

_____

_____

_____

_____

Why we wanted to do this:

_____

_____

_____

Thoughts/Memories:

_____

_____

_____

_____

_____

_____

_____

_____

_____

_____

≫≫————➤ ≫≫————➤ ≫≫————➤ ≫≫————➤

_____

Date Completed:_____

Overall Rating: ☆ ☆ ☆ ☆ ☆

Description:

_____

_____

_____

_____

_____

Why we wanted to do this:

_____

_____

_____

Thoughts/Memories:

_____

_____

_____

_____

_____

_____

_____

_____

_____

_____

_____

>>>———➤ >>>———➤ >>>———➤ >>>———➤

Date Completed:_____

Overall Rating: ☆ ☆ ☆ ☆ ☆

Description:

_____
_____
_____
_____
_____

Why we wanted to do this:

_____
_____
_____

Thoughts/Memories:

_____
_____
_____
_____
_____
_____
_____
_____
_____

Date Completed:_____

Overall Rating: ☆ ☆ ☆ ☆ ☆

Description:

_____
_____
_____
_____
_____

Why we wanted to do this:

_____
_____
_____

Thoughts/Memories:

_____
_____
_____
_____
_____
_____
_____
_____
_____
_____

⟫⟫⟫———➤ ⟫⟫⟫———➤ ⟫⟫⟫———➤ ⟫⟫⟫———➤

Date Completed:_____

Overall Rating: ☆ ☆ ☆ ☆ ☆

Description:

_____
_____
_____
_____
_____

Why we wanted to do this:

_____
_____
_____

Thoughts/Memories:

_____
_____
_____
_____
_____
_____
_____
_____
_____
_____

⟫⟫⟫———➤ ⟫⟫⟫———➤ ⟫⟫⟫———➤ ⟫⟫⟫———➤

_____

Date Completed:_____

Overall Rating: ☆ ☆ ☆ ☆ ☆

Description:

_____

_____

_____

_____

_____

Why we wanted to do this:

_____

_____

_____

Thoughts/Memories:

_____

_____

_____

_____

_____

_____

_____

_____

_____

>>>————➤ >>>————➤ >>>————➤ >>>————➤

Date Completed:_____

Overall Rating: ☆ ☆ ☆ ☆ ☆

Description:

_____
_____
_____
_____
_____

Why we wanted to do this:

_____
_____
_____

Thoughts/Memories:

_____
_____
_____
_____
_____
_____
_____
_____
_____
_____
_____

»»———➤ »»———➤ »»———➤ »»———➤

Date Completed:_____

Overall Rating: ☆ ☆ ☆ ☆ ☆

Description:

_____

_____

_____

_____

_____

Why we wanted to do this:

_____

_____

_____

Thoughts/Memories:

_____

_____

_____

_____

_____

_____

_____

_____

_____

_____

≫≫—→ ≫≫—→ ≫≫—→ ≫≫—→

Date Completed:_____

Overall Rating: ☆ ☆ ☆ ☆ ☆

Description:

_____
_____
_____
_____
_____

Why we wanted to do this:

_____
_____
_____

Thoughts/Memories:

_____
_____
_____
_____
_____
_____
_____
_____
_____
_____
_____

>>>———► >>>———► >>>———► >>>———►

Date Completed: _____

Overall Rating: ☆ ☆ ☆ ☆ ☆

Description:

_____

_____

_____

_____

_____

Why we wanted to do this:

_____

_____

_____

Thoughts/Memories:

_____

_____

_____

_____

_____

_____

_____

_____

_____

_____

》》》———→ 》》》———→ 》》》———→ 》》》———→

Date Completed:_____

Overall Rating: ☆ ☆ ☆ ☆ ☆

Description:

_____

_____

_____

_____

_____

Why we wanted to do this:

_____

_____

_____

Thoughts/Memories:

_____

_____

_____

_____

_____

_____

_____

_____

_____

_____

_____

⟫⟫⟫———➤ ⟫⟫⟫———➤ ⟫⟫⟫———➤ ⟫⟫⟫———➤

Date Completed:_____

Overall Rating: ☆ ☆ ☆ ☆ ☆

Description:

_____

_____

_____

_____

_____

Why we wanted to do this:

_____

_____

_____

Thoughts/Memories:

_____

_____

_____

_____

_____

_____

_____

_____

_____

_____

》》》——➤ 》》》——➤   》》》——➤   》》》——➤

_____

Date Completed:_____

Overall Rating: ☆ ☆ ☆ ☆ ☆

Description:

_____
_____
_____
_____
_____

Why we wanted to do this:

_____
_____
_____

Thoughts/Memories:

_____
_____
_____
_____
_____
_____
_____
_____
_____
_____
_____

≫≫⟶ ≫≫⟶ ≫≫⟶ ≫≫⟶

Date Completed:_____

Overall Rating: ☆ ☆ ☆ ☆ ☆

Description:

_____
_____
_____
_____
_____

Why we wanted to do this:

_____
_____
_____

Thoughts/Memories:

_____
_____
_____
_____
_____
_____
_____
_____
_____

》》》———➤ 》》》———➤ 》》》———➤ 》》》———➤

Date Completed: _____

Overall Rating: ☆ ☆ ☆ ☆ ☆

Description:

_____

_____

_____

_____

_____

Why we wanted to do this:

_____

_____

_____

Thoughts/Memories:

_____

_____

_____

_____

_____

_____

_____

_____

_____

_____

Date Completed:_____

Overall Rating: ☆ ☆ ☆ ☆ ☆

Description:

_____

_____

_____

_____

_____

Why we wanted to do this:

_____

_____

_____

Thoughts/Memories:

_____

_____

_____

_____

_____

_____

_____

_____

_____

_____

_____

Date Completed: _____

Overall Rating: ☆ ☆ ☆ ☆ ☆

Description:

_____
_____
_____
_____
_____

Why we wanted to do this:

_____
_____
_____

Thoughts/Memories:

_____
_____
_____
_____
_____
_____
_____
_____
_____
_____
_____

»»———➤ »»———➤ »»———➤ »»———➤

Date Completed: _____

Overall Rating: ☆ ☆ ☆ ☆ ☆

Description:

_____
_____
_____
_____
_____

Why we wanted to do this:

_____
_____
_____

Thoughts/Memories:

_____
_____
_____
_____
_____
_____
_____
_____
_____
_____

≫》━━➤ ≫》━━➤ ≫》━━➤ ≫》━━➤

_____

Date Completed:_____

Overall Rating: ☆ ☆ ☆ ☆ ☆

Description:

_____
_____
_____
_____
_____

Why we wanted to do this:

_____
_____
_____

Thoughts/Memories:

_____
_____
_____
_____
_____
_____
_____
_____
_____
_____
_____

⟫⟫⟶   ⟫⟫⟶   ⟫⟫⟶   ⟫⟫⟶

Date Completed:_____

Overall Rating: ☆ ☆ ☆ ☆ ☆

Description:

_____
_____
_____
_____
_____

Why we wanted to do this:

_____
_____
_____

Thoughts/Memories:

_____
_____
_____
_____
_____
_____
_____
_____
_____
_____

》》》 ⟶ 》》》 ⟶ 》》》 ⟶ 》》》 ⟶

Date Completed:_____

Overall Rating: ☆ ☆ ☆ ☆ ☆

Description:

_____
_____
_____
_____
_____

Why we wanted to do this:

_____
_____
_____

Thoughts/Memories:

_____
_____
_____
_____
_____
_____
_____
_____
_____
_____

Date Completed:_____

Overall Rating: ☆ ☆ ☆ ☆ ☆

Description:

_____
_____
_____
_____
_____

Why we wanted to do this:

_____
_____
_____

Thoughts/Memories:

_____
_____
_____
_____
_____
_____
_____
_____
_____
_____

》》》———➤ 》》》———➤ 》》》———➤ 》》》———➤

Date Completed:_____

Overall Rating: ☆ ☆ ☆ ☆ ☆

Description:

_____
_____
_____
_____
_____

Why we wanted to do this:

_____
_____
_____

Thoughts/Memories:

_____
_____
_____
_____
_____
_____
_____
_____
_____
_____

»»——➤ »»——➤ »»——➤ »»——➤

Date Completed:_____

Overall Rating: ☆ ☆ ☆ ☆ ☆

Description:

_____

_____

_____

_____

_____

Why we wanted to do this:

_____

_____

_____

Thoughts/Memories:

_____

_____

_____

_____

_____

_____

_____

_____

_____

_____

》》》————➤ 》》》————➤ 》》》————➤ 》》》————➤

Date Completed:_____

Overall Rating: ☆ ☆ ☆ ☆ ☆

Description:

_____
_____
_____
_____
_____

Why we wanted to do this:

_____
_____
_____

Thoughts/Memories:

_____
_____
_____
_____
_____
_____
_____
_____
_____
_____
_____

_____

Date Completed: _____

Overall Rating: ☆ ☆ ☆ ☆ ☆

Description:

_____

_____

_____

_____

_____

Why we wanted to do this:

_____

_____

_____

Thoughts/Memories:

_____

_____

_____

_____

_____

_____

_____

_____

_____

_____

_____

》》》———➤ 》》》———➤ 》》》———➤ 》》》———➤

Date Completed:_____

Overall Rating: ☆ ☆ ☆ ☆ ☆

Description:

_____
_____
_____
_____
_____

Why we wanted to do this:

_____
_____
_____

Thoughts/Memories:

_____
_____
_____
_____
_____
_____
_____
_____
_____
_____
_____

»»——► »»——► »»——► »»——►

Date Completed:_____

Overall Rating: ☆ ☆ ☆ ☆ ☆

Description:

_____
_____
_____
_____
_____

Why we wanted to do this:

_____
_____
_____

Thoughts/Memories:

_____
_____
_____
_____
_____
_____
_____
_____
_____
_____
_____

≫≫—→ ≫≫—→ ≫≫—→ ≫≫—→

Date Completed: _____

Overall Rating: ☆ ☆ ☆ ☆ ☆

Description:

_____
_____
_____
_____
_____

Why we wanted to do this:

_____
_____
_____

Thoughts/Memories:

_____
_____
_____
_____
_____
_____
_____
_____
_____
_____
_____

Date Completed:_____

Overall Rating: ☆ ☆ ☆ ☆ ☆

Description:

_____
_____
_____
_____
_____

Why we wanted to do this:

_____
_____
_____

Thoughts/Memories:

_____
_____
_____
_____
_____
_____
_____
_____
_____
_____
_____

》》》———➤ 》》》———➤ 》》》———➤ 》》》———➤

Date Completed:_____

Overall Rating: ☆ ☆ ☆ ☆ ☆

Description:

_____
_____
_____
_____
_____

Why we wanted to do this:

_____
_____
_____

Thoughts/Memories:

_____
_____
_____
_____
_____
_____
_____
_____
_____
_____

Date Completed:_____

Overall Rating: ☆ ☆ ☆ ☆ ☆

Description:

_____
_____
_____
_____
_____

Why we wanted to do this:

_____
_____
_____

Thoughts/Memories:

_____
_____
_____
_____
_____
_____
_____
_____
_____
_____
_____

>>>———➤ >>>———➤ >>>———➤ >>>———➤

Date Completed:_____

Overall Rating: ☆ ☆ ☆ ☆ ☆

Description:

_____
_____
_____
_____
_____

Why we wanted to do this:

_____
_____
_____

Thoughts/Memories:

_____
_____
_____
_____
_____
_____
_____
_____
_____
_____
_____
_____

➤➤➤—➤ ➤➤➤—➤ ➤➤➤—➤ ➤➤➤—➤

Date Completed: _____

Overall Rating: ☆ ☆ ☆ ☆ ☆

Description:

_____
_____
_____
_____
_____

Why we wanted to do this:

_____
_____
_____

Thoughts/Memories:

_____
_____
_____
_____
_____
_____
_____
_____
_____
_____

》》》———▶ 》》》———▶ 》》》———▶ 》》》———▶

Date Completed:_____

Overall Rating: ☆ ☆ ☆ ☆ ☆

Description:

_____
_____
_____
_____
_____

Why we wanted to do this:

_____
_____
_____

Thoughts/Memories:

_____
_____
_____
_____
_____
_____
_____
_____
_____
_____

Date Completed:_____

Overall Rating: ☆ ☆ ☆ ☆ ☆

Description:

_____
_____
_____
_____
_____

Why we wanted to do this:

_____
_____
_____

Thoughts/Memories:

_____
_____
_____
_____
_____
_____
_____
_____
_____
_____

»»» ——➤ »»» ——➤ »»» ——➤ »»» ——➤

Date Completed:_____

Overall Rating: ☆ ☆ ☆ ☆ ☆

Description:

_____
_____
_____
_____
_____

Why we wanted to do this:

_____
_____
_____

Thoughts/Memories:

_____
_____
_____
_____
_____
_____
_____
_____
_____
_____
_____

Date Completed:_____

Overall Rating: ☆ ☆ ☆ ☆ ☆

Description:

_____
_____
_____
_____
_____

Why we wanted to do this:

_____
_____
_____

Thoughts/Memories:

_____
_____
_____
_____
_____
_____
_____
_____
_____

》》》——→ 》》》——→ 》》》——→ 》》》——→

Date Completed:_____

Overall Rating: ☆ ☆ ☆ ☆ ☆

Description:

_____
_____
_____
_____
_____

Why we wanted to do this:

_____
_____
_____

Thoughts/Memories:

_____
_____
_____
_____
_____
_____
_____
_____
_____
_____
_____

_____

Date Completed:_____

Overall Rating: ☆ ☆ ☆ ☆ ☆

Description:

_____

_____

_____

_____

_____

Why we wanted to do this:

_____

_____

_____

Thoughts/Memories:

_____

_____

_____

_____

_____

_____

_____

_____

_____

_____

⫸⟶ ⫸⟶ ⫸⟶ ⫸⟶

Date Completed:_____

Overall Rating: ☆ ☆ ☆ ☆ ☆

Description:

_____
_____
_____
_____
_____

Why we wanted to do this:

_____
_____
_____

Thoughts/Memories:

_____
_____
_____
_____
_____
_____
_____
_____
_____
_____
_____

Date Completed:_____

Overall Rating: ☆ ☆ ☆ ☆ ☆

Description:

_____
_____
_____
_____
_____

Why we wanted to do this:

_____
_____
_____

Thoughts/Memories:

_____
_____
_____
_____
_____
_____
_____
_____
_____
_____

≫≫——➤ ≫≫——➤ ≫≫——➤ ≫≫——➤

Date Completed:_____

Overall Rating: ☆ ☆ ☆ ☆ ☆

Description:

_____
_____
_____
_____
_____

Why we wanted to do this:

_____
_____
_____

Thoughts/Memories:

_____
_____
_____
_____
_____
_____
_____
_____
_____
_____
_____

》》》———➤ 》》》———➤   》》》———➤ 》》》———➤

Date Completed:_____

Overall Rating: ☆ ☆ ☆ ☆ ☆

Description:

_____
_____
_____
_____
_____

Why we wanted to do this:

_____
_____
_____

Thoughts/Memories:

_____
_____
_____
_____
_____
_____
_____
_____
_____
_____

>>>———▶ >>>———▶ >>>———▶ >>>———▶

Date Completed:_____

Overall Rating: ☆ ☆ ☆ ☆ ☆

Description:

_____
_____
_____
_____
_____

Why we wanted to do this:

_____
_____
_____

Thoughts/Memories:

_____
_____
_____
_____
_____
_____
_____
_____
_____
_____

》》》———➤ 》》》———➤ 》》》———➤ 》》》———➤

Date Completed:_____

Overall Rating: ☆ ☆ ☆ ☆ ☆

Description:

_____
_____
_____
_____
_____

Why we wanted to do this:

_____
_____
_____

Thoughts/Memories:

_____
_____
_____
_____
_____
_____
_____
_____
_____
_____
_____

》》 ➤ 》》 ➤ 》》 ➤ 》》 ➤

Date Completed:_____

Overall Rating: ☆ ☆ ☆ ☆ ☆

Description:

_____
_____
_____
_____
_____

Why we wanted to do this:

_____
_____
_____

Thoughts/Memories:

_____
_____
_____
_____
_____
_____
_____
_____
_____
_____
_____

≫≫—➤ ≫≫—➤ ≫≫—➤ ≫≫—➤

Date Completed:_____

Overall Rating: ☆ ☆ ☆ ☆ ☆

Description:

_____
_____
_____
_____
_____

Why we wanted to do this:

_____
_____
_____

Thoughts/Memories:

_____
_____
_____
_____
_____
_____
_____
_____
_____
_____

》》》————➤ 》》》————➤ 》》》————➤ 》》》————➤

Date Completed:_____

Overall Rating: ☆ ☆ ☆ ☆ ☆

Description:

_____
_____
_____
_____
_____

Why we wanted to do this:

_____
_____
_____

Thoughts/Memories:

_____
_____
_____
_____
_____
_____
_____
_____
_____
_____

Date Completed: _____

Overall Rating: ☆ ☆ ☆ ☆ ☆

Description:

_____
_____
_____
_____
_____

Why we wanted to do this:

_____
_____
_____

Thoughts/Memories:

_____
_____
_____
_____
_____
_____
_____
_____
_____
_____

》》》————➤ 》》》————➤ 》》》————➤ 》》》————➤

Date Completed:_____

Overall Rating: ☆ ☆ ☆ ☆ ☆

Description:

_____
_____
_____
_____
_____

Why we wanted to do this:

_____
_____
_____

Thoughts/Memories:

_____
_____
_____
_____
_____
_____
_____
_____
_____
_____

>>>———➤ >>>———➤ >>>———➤ >>>———➤

Date Completed:_____

Overall Rating: ☆ ☆ ☆ ☆ ☆

Description:

_____

_____

_____

_____

_____

Why we wanted to do this:

_____

_____

_____

Thoughts/Memories:

_____

_____

_____

_____

_____

_____

_____

_____

_____

_____

_____

>>>———➤   >>>———➤   >>>———➤   >>>———➤

Date Completed:_____

Overall Rating: ☆ ☆ ☆ ☆ ☆

Description:

_____
_____
_____
_____
_____

Why we wanted to do this:

_____
_____
_____

Thoughts/Memories:

_____
_____
_____
_____
_____
_____
_____
_____
_____
_____

Date Completed:_____

Overall Rating: ☆ ☆ ☆ ☆ ☆

Description:

_____

_____

_____

_____

_____

Why we wanted to do this:

_____

_____

_____

Thoughts/Memories:

_____

_____

_____

_____

_____

_____

_____

_____

_____

_____

》》》 ➤ 》》》 ➤ 》》》 ➤ 》》》 ➤

_____

Date Completed:_____

Overall Rating: ☆ ☆ ☆ ☆ ☆

Description:

_____
_____
_____
_____
_____

Why we wanted to do this:

_____
_____
_____

Thoughts/Memories:

_____
_____
_____
_____
_____
_____
_____
_____
_____
_____
_____

»»———➤ »»———➤ »»———➤ »»———➤

101 bucket list ideas

1. Ride in a hot air balloon
✓ 2. Visit each other's home towns and give tours
3. Research and record your family trees
4. Learn how to say "I love you" in at least 5 languages
5. Go on an overnight train trip
✓ 6. Visit a haunted mansion
✓ 7. Visit a castle
8. Write a song together, even if it's silly and neither of you can sing
9. Create code words for party escapes, I love you's, having a bad day, or anything else
10. Grow a vegetable garden together
✓ 11. Go deep sea fishing or whale watching
12. Ride a tandem bicycle
✓ 13. Go to a remote island or location
✓ 14. Learn a new language together
✓ 15. Stay at a bed and breakfast
16. Kiss under a waterfall
17. Take an unplanned overnight road trip
18. Dance in the rain
✓ 19. Kiss on the top of a ferris wheel ride
✓ 20. Get a couples massage
✓ 21. Go bowling
22. Create a signature impressive meal together or take a cooking class together
23. Ride horses on the beach
24. Go to a nude beach
✓ 25. Go to a wine tasting
✓ 26. Pick your own fruit at an orchard and make something with it
27. Make life goals together
28. Write a love poem together or to each other
✓ 29. Try each other's hobbies
30. Wear matching outfits in public
✓ 31. Watch a meteor shower
✓ 32. Write cute sweet notes or texts weekly
33. Have a tradition for every holiday
✓ 34. Learn a line dance together or some other synchronized dance
✓ 35. Volunteer to do something together

101 bucket list ideas

36. ✓ Take dance lessons together
37. ✓ Teach each other something
38. ✓ Have sex in the water (ocean, pool, hot tub or shower)
39.   Make love in every room of your house
40.   Recreate your first date or proposal
41. ✓ Hang out together in a hammock
42. ✓ Go snorkeling
43. ✓ Sing together – go Christmas caroling or do karaoke
44.   Go white water rafting
45.   Go camping and sleep in a tent
46. ✓ Kiss in front of the Eiffel tower
47.   Say I love you in a gondola
48. ✓ Swim with dolphins, stingrays or sharks
49. ✓ Watch a volcano erupt
50.   See the northern lights
51.   Watch the sunrise and sunset in the same day
52.   Attend and bet on a horse race
53. ✓ Get your palms or futures read
54.   Hunt for mushrooms
55. ✓ Try the most exotic foods on the menu in a different country
56.   Meet each other for a date in disguise
57.   Donate blood together
58. ✓ Attend a professional athletic event
59. ✓ Feed each other gourmet desserts
60.   Visit every continent
61. ✓ Complete a corn maze
62.   Go indoor skydiving
63.   Take a helicopter tour
64. ✓ Attend a major festival or event (Mardi Gras, New Year's Eve, Burning Man)
65.   Spend a weekend away with no electronic devices
66.   Swim in every ocean
67. ✓ Go bird watching
68.   Do tandem parasailing
69.   Get cartoon images drawn of yourselves
70. ✓ Pack and go on a picnic
71.   Race go carts or bumper cars

101 bucket list ideas

72. √ Stargaze somewhere amazing
73. √ Ride a river boat
74.   Paddleboard or surf together
75. √ Relax in a hot springs
76.   Go on a safari
77. √ Visit a cathedral
78. √ Complete a jigsaw puzzle together
79. √ Have a candlelight dinner for no reason
80. √ Try out local food trucks
81.   Tour all of your local attractions
82.   Watch a double feature movie matinee
83. √ Go bowling, roller skating or ice skating
84.   Ride a mechanical bull
85.   Go geocaching
86. √ Fly kites together
87.   Get pedicures together
88.   Play paintball or laser tag
89. √ Design your own plates at a pottery studio
90. √ Go to a local musical show, concert or play
91. √ Feed the ducks
92.   Complete a crossword puzzle together
93. √ Go to a farmers market
94. √ Play strip poker
95. √ Build a sandcastle together
96.   Learn a magic trick together
97.   Rent a convertible
98. √ Attend an amazing fireworks display
99.   Make your own wine, beer, cider, kombucha or create and name your own signatures beverage
100. √ Play at the playground of a loyal park
101. √ Skip rocks

Made in the USA
San Bernardino, CA
04 December 2018